THE DISPARITY PHILOSOPHY BETWEEN CULPABLE HOMICIDE AND MURDER IN THE INDIAN PENAL CODE

VOLUME 1, ISSUE 3 OF BRAIN BOOSTER ARTICLES

SUBHAJIT SAMANTA

Contents

Preface

"Start writing, no matter what. The water does not flow until the faucet is turned on".

-Louis L'Amour

Hundreds of students and professors are contributing their work to Brain Booster Articles, we are here to provide ample information about Law and Contemporary issues. Our aim is to provide a platform for today's generation to express their views and ideas on law and contemporary law.

Publication

This research paper is published in volume 1, issue 3 of Brain Booster
Articles

Author

CHAPTER ONE

ABSTRACT

The section 299 and 300, IPC deal with the explanation of Culpable Homicide and murder. The basic term of culpable homicide as manslaughter under the English law which is the 'genius' and murder which is a 'species' of the culpable homicide. According to section 299 of IPC that would be an offence when any person is causing death with the intention of causing death or by creating any bodily harm of a human being. Besides, the section 300 of IPC is considered to be an offence which against any human body or it is done with actual intention to confer the harm. This is a common distinction between culpable homicide and murder. In reality there is a very thin line of distinction between the two postulations. The section 304 confers the punishment for culpable homicide is not amounting to murder which may extend imprisonment to ten years and shall also be liable to fine as well as section 302 confers the punishment for murder which shall be punished with death or imprisonment for life and shall also be liable to fine. This paper aims to evaluate vis-a-vis culpable homicide and murder grounds as well as judicial perspectives on the concern.

CHAPTER TWO

INTRODUCTION

"Every murder or other injury, no matter for what cause, committed or inflicted on another is a crime against humanity".
-Mahatma Gandhi.[1]

The concept of culpable homicide and murder are the most complicated provisions under the Indian Penal Code. The culpable homicide and murder scrupulously resembling each other and at times it has been very difficult to pick out between the two provisions as the committing of death is common to both. Moreover, there should necessarily be criminal intention or knowledge in both culpable homicide and murder. However, the difference between culpable homicide and murder is actual based upon a very elusive distinction of the intention and knowledge which involved in these crimes. Though, the difference repossess in the degree where the greater intention or knowledge of the fatal is caused and the liability, nature and punishment of the act incurred for both are different. It is seen that any conduct which harms an individual that would be harm for the entire society as this society is invented of individuals and thus it is exactly said about crime that it is an offence against the society.

[1] Mahatma Gandhi (2005). "All Men Are Brothers", p.81, A&C Black.

CHAPTER THREE

THE CONCEPT OF CULPABLE HOMICIDE

It is the highest order of bodily injury that can be inflicted on a human body. Since the earliest time it has been considered the most heinous offence which means the killing of a human being by a human being, however, in every case of killing is not culpable. There might be cases where the law would not punish a man for committing homicide such as killing for self-defense, pursuance of a lawful authority or reason of mistake of facts are not culpable. Similarly, if death is caused by accident or any misfortune and while doing an act bonafide and has no intention to killed such person and the man would be excused to criminal responsibility for homicide. Besides, if the killing is not legally justified the man would be liable for that as per law. Even though, if a foreigner enemy is killed save in the operation of war then the killing would be punishable as the killing of any other man.[1]

THE ESSENTIAL INGREDIENTS OF CULPABLE HOMICIDE

1. **By causing death of person other than person whose death was intended**

In order to hold a person liable under the impeached section there must be causing of death of a human being as laid down under section 46 of the Code. The causing of death of a child in the mother's womb is not homicide as put in explanation 3 conjoin to section 299, IPC. However, the person would not be set free and would be punishable for causing miscarriage either under section 312 or 315 of IPC depending on the gravity of the injury. The act of causing death amounts to culpable homicide if any part of that child has been brought forth, though the child may not have breathed or been entirely born. The clause 'though the child may not have breathed' recommends that a child may be born alive, though it may not breath or it may anaerobic so that imperfectly that it may be difficult to acquire clear proof that respiration has grasped place and causing of death ought to be of a living human being which means a living man, woman, child and at least partially an infant under delivery or just delivered.

To attract the provisions of this section it adequately if the death of a human being is caused whether the person was intended to be killed or not. For example, A counsels as per acquires poison to A and confers it to his mother in a roasted apple. The mother confers the apple to a child of B and not knowledge that it has made by poison and the child eats it and dies. In the circumstance A would amount to murder by B though he never intended to kill the child according to section 301, IPC. In *Public Prosecutor v. MS Moorty*[2] the accused with the intention of killing A. *Narasimhulu* (on whose life he had taken out considerable insurance without the latter's knowledge) in order to acquire the corroborated amount conferred him some sweets mixed with poison. The intended victim ate some of the sweets and launch the rest away which were picked up by two children who ate them and died of poisoning. Though the accused was liable for the murder of the children though he intended merely to kill *Narasimhulu*.

2. **By doing an Act**

The death may be occurred by a hundred and one means, such as by poisoning, drowning, striking and beating. As laid down under section 32, IPC the word 'act' has been conferred a extensive meaning in the Code considering as it includes not merely an act of commission, however, illegal omissions as well. Hence, death may also be caused by neglect of duty such as a parent not supplying food and medical care to his child, a husband famishing his wife that results in the voluntary causing of the child's and wife's death.[3] For instance, *A omits to confer Z food and by that omission voluntarily causes Z's death. Is this murder? According our rule it is murder, if A was Z's directed by the law to embellish Z with food. It is murder if Z was the infant child of A. Therefore, had a legal right to comestible which right a Civil Court would enforce against A. It is murder if Z was a incapacitated invalid and A, a nurse was hired to feed Z. It is murder if A was detaining Z in unlawful confinement. Thus, contracted a legal obligation to embellish Z, during the continuance of the confinement with the necessaries. It is not murder if Z is a beggar who has no other claim on A than that of humanity.*[4]

3. Knowledge as Mens rea

As it has been stated earlier that the third degree of intention contemplated under the definition of culpable homicide is knowledge. The third part of section 299 confers "whoever causes death by doing an act with the knowledge that he is likely by such act to cause death and commits the offence of culpable homicide". In the scheme of the section that the least or minimum degree of mental element contemplated to make an act of homicide culpable is the knowledge that the act is likely to cause death.

However, the knowledge means consciousness and it denotes a state of conscious awareness of certain facts in which human mind remains inactive. Besides, it connotes a bare awareness of the consequences of his conduct[5]. The offender should reasonably expect that the consequence of his act would probably result in the death of a person even if he did not intend to cause the death."[6] The word "likely" as used in section 299 is to denote a lower degree of likelihood whereas the same word "likely" in section 300 would denote a higher degree of likelihood of death. The word "likely" in section 299 conveys the sense of probability as distinguished from merely possibility or probability.[7]

[1]I Hale PC 433.
[2]Public Prosecutor v. MS Moorty,1912, 13 Cr LJ 145 (146) (Mad).
[3]Om Prakash V. State of Punjab, AIR 1961, SC 1782.
[4]Draft Penal Code, note M, pp. 138-139.
[5]Jai Prakash v. State of Delhi, (1991) 2 SCC 32.
[6]TakhajiHiraji v. Thakore KubersingChamansing, AIR 2001, SC 2328.
[7]Raj Pal v. State of Haryana, (2006) 9 SCC 678.

CHAPTER FOUR

THE CONCEPT OF MURDER

The word 'murder' was derived from the Germanic word 'mortna' which means secret killing. According to early Germanic people there was a distinction between open killing and secret killing. Since 12th century every homicide whether open or secret was considered to be recognised as grave and made punishable. Under English law unlawful homicide may broadly be classified into murder and manslaughter.[1]

Though, the murder has not been defined in India by its legislature. Though, under English law it is generally said to be committed "when a person of sound mind and discretion unlawfully kills any reasonable creature in being and under King's peace, with malice aforethought either express or implied".On the other hand, the manslaughter is said to be an 'unlawful killing of such a person without malice either express or implied.[2]

The offence of 'murder' is an aggravated form of 'culpable homicide'. The section 300 of the IPC confers that when the offence is 'murder' and when it is 'culpable homicide not amounting to murder'. The section 300, IPC commences by setting out the circumstances when culpable homicide turns into murder which is punishable under section 302, IPC and the exceptions in the same section confers that when the offence is not murder, however, is culpable homicide not amounting to murder punishable under the first part of section 304, IPC.

In other words, the culpable homicide is murder if the act by which death is caused falls within any one of the four clauses mentioned in the section, until the case comes under one of the five exceptions stated therein, when the offence will amount to 'culpable homicide not amounting to murder'. These are the cases wherein death is caused whilst the accused is deprived of the power of self-control by grave and sudden provocation or in the course of exercising the right of private defence or in the exercise of legal powers or in a sudden fight or with the consent of the deceased.

[1]Pollock and Maitland History of English Law, 2nd Edn, Vol. II, p. 487.

[2]Kenny's Outlines of Criminal Law, 19th Edn. J.W.C. Turner, (1966), p. 147.

CHAPTER FIVE

THE DISTINGUISHED BETWEEN CULPABLE HOMICIDE AND MURDER

According to Sir James Stephen definition of culpable homicide and murder are the weakest part of the IPC as they are defined in forms closely resembling each other and at times it becomes difficult to distinguish between the two as the causing of death is common to both. Moreover, there must necessarily be criminal intention or knowledge in both culpable homicide and murder. However, the difference between culpable homicide and murder is real though very fine and based upon a very subtle distinction of the intention and knowledge involved in these crimes. The true difference lies in the degree and there being the greater intention or knowledge of the fatal consequences in the one case than the other. The four cases describing the offence under section 300, IPC attempt to laid dwon this difference.

In *Reg v. Govinda,*[1] the judgement of Melville laid down the distinction between culpable homicide and murder could be well appreciated by the illustration. The prisoner was a young man of 18 and he kicked his wife who was a girl of 15 and struck her several times with his fist on the back. These blows seemed to have caused her no serious injury. However, she fell on the ground and then the accused put one knee on her chest and struck her two or three times on the face. One or two of these blows were violent and took effect on the girl's left eye, producing contusion (injury without breaking skin) and discolouration. The skull was not fractured but the blow caused extravasation of blood in the brain and the girl died in consequence either on the spot or very shortly afterwards. The Sessions Judge and the assessors found the prisoner guilty of murder and sentenced him to death.

The case was sent up to the High Court of Bombay for confirmation of the sentence of death passed on the prisoner. There being a difference of opinion between the judges of the Bombay High Court as to what offence the prisoner had committed that the case was referred to a third judge, Melville, J. for convenience of comparison the provisions of sections 299 and 300 of the Indian Penal Code may be stated thus:

Section 299, IPC (Culpable Homicide)	Section 300, IPC (Murder)
A person commits culpable homicide if the act by which the death is caused is done.	The subject to certain exceptions, culpable homicide is murder, if the act by which the death is caused is done
(a) With the intention of causing death.	(1) With the intention of causing death.
	(2) With the intention of causing such bodily injury, as the offender *knows to be likely to cause the death of the to whom the harm is caused.*
(b) With the intention of causing such bodily injury as is likely to cause death.	(3) With the intention of causing bodily injury to any person, and the bodily injury intended to be inflicted is sufficient in the ordinary course of nature to cause death.
	(4) With the knowledge that the act

(c) With the knowledge that the act is likely to cause death.	is so imminently dangerous that it must in all probability cause death or such bodily injury as is likely to cause death and committed without excuse for any incurring the risk or causing death or such injury as aforesaid.

[1]Reg v. Govinda, 1876 ILR 1 Bom 342.

CHAPTER SIX

WHEN THE CULPABLE HOMICIDE IS NOT AMOUNTING TO MURDER?

A. Grave and Sudden Provocation

It is the most important which has perplexed the courts from time to time what amounts to grave and sudden provocation in repercussion of which the accused is deprived of his power of self-control which will entitle him to the sake of the exception. The answer to this depends on a number of factors and It is mainly a question of fact to be marked according to the facts and circumstances of each case. The scope of the doctrine of provocation has been well-stated by Simon L.C. in the case of *Mancini v. Director of Public Prosecutions*[1] It is not all provocation that would diminish the crime of murder to manslaughter (culpable homicide). The provocation to have that consequence which must be such as temporarily divests a person provoked of the power of self-control as a result of which he commits the unlawful act which causes death. The test to be applied is that of the effect of the provocation on a reasonable man as was explained by the Court of Criminal Appeal in *Rex v. Lesbini*[2] thus, an unusually mercurial or antagonistic individual is not entitled to rely on provocation which would not have led an ordinary person to act as he did.

In applying the test it is of particular importance to:

a. To consider whether a sufficient interval has elapsed since the provocation to allow a reasonable man time to cool.

b. To take into account the instrument with which the homicide was effected. To retort, in the heat of passion induced by provocation and a simple blow that is a very different thing from making use of a deadly instrument such as a enshrouded dagger. In short, the mode of indignation must bear a reasonable relationship to the provocation if the offence is to be reduced to manslaughter.

B. Exceeding the Right of Private Defence

This exception confers that a person may exceed the right of private defence if the excess is intentional the offence is murder or unintentional then it would be culpable homicide not amounting to murder. Besides, if the accused caused the death of a person without pre-planning and that when the accused committed the death of the deceased and he has no intention of causing more harm than was necessary for the purpose of defence (even if he caused more harm than was necessary for the purpose of private defence) and that the act was done in good faith.

For instance, A man who voluntarily kills another for prevent other from pulling his nose ought to be allowed to go absolutely unpunished and it would be most dangerous. The law shall punish and ought to punish such killing, however, we would not think that the law should punish such killing as murder for the law itself has encouraged the slayer to inflict on the assailant any harm short of death which may be necessary for the impetus of repelling the disapproval to confer the assailant a cut with a knife across the fingers which may render his right hand useless of him for life or to hurt him downstairs with such force as to break his leg and it seems difficult to draw up that circumstances which would be a full justification of any violence short of homicide should not be a mitigation of the guilt of homicide. That a man should be merely exercising a right by fracturing the skull and knocking out the eye of an assailant and would be guilty of the highest crime in the Code if he kills the same assailant that there would be merely a single step between perfect innocence and murder, between perfect indemnity and liability to capital punishment and it seems unreasonable. In a case in which the law itself empowers an individual to inflict any harm short of death and it ought hardly to visit him with the highest punishment if he inflicts death.[3]

It is a cardinal principle of the law of right of private defence that the accused must be free from fault in bringing about an encounter; there must be present an impending peril to life or of great bodily harm, either real or apparent, such as to create an honest belief of an existing necessity; there must be no safe or reasonable mode of escape by retreat and there must be a genuine need for taking life.[4] The right of private defence is purely preventive and not punitive or retributive.[5]

C. **Public servant exceeding his powers**

This Exception has been provided to protect a public servant or a person assisting a public servant if either of them exceeds the power conferred for the advancement of public justice. This exception would not apply if the act is illegal or against public policy and not authorised by law or the person blazingly exceeds the power given to him by law. The question whether the public officer did or did not belief in the legality of his powers is a question of fact to be decided upon the facts and circumstances of each case. In *Dukhi Singh v. State[6]* the appellant, a constable of the RPF (Railway Protection Force) while on duty arrested a man under suspicious circumstances who was standing near a goods wagon while the train had ended at Hadlda Khas Station near Allahabad and took him to his compartment. When the train had moved a few paces the arrested man jumped down from it. As soon as he escaped the appellant followed him with a rifle and suspecting that the train fireman had concealed the thief he enquired from the fireman where the culprit was and further said that he would shoot him. The fireman asked the appellant why he would shoot the thief afterward the appellant shot him with his rifle. The fireman later died.

The appellant supplicated that he had been conferred orders by Havildar Kashi Singh to shoot at the thief and further asserted at it was a case of pure accident that instead of hitting the thief he hit the fireman. Held that in effecting his arrest after the get away the police officer had not had the right to cause the death of the suspected thief. Further held, that the appellant exceeded the powers conferred to him by law and he caused the death of the fireman by doing an act which he bonafide believed to be lawful and necessary for the due to discharge of his duty and the case would be covered by exception 3 to section 300 of the Indian Penal Code. In such circumstances the offence that was committed culpable homicide not amounting to murder which punishable under section 304.

D. **Without Premeditation in a sudden fight**

This exception applies to cases wherein death is committed in a sudden fight without pre-planning in the heat of passion upon a sudden quarrel so long as the fight is unpremeditated and sudden that the accused and irrespective of his conduct before the quarrel earns the mitigation conferred for in exception 4 to section 300, IPC subject to the condition that he did not in the course of the fight take undue advantage of or act in a cruel or unusual manner.[7] The most crucial element under this clause that there ought be a sudden fight. The word 'fight' has not been explained in the Code. In ordinary used the word 'fight' means a conflict between two or more persons whether with or without weapons. However, a mere verbal exchange of words preceding a stab with a knife will not invoke the application of exception 4 to section 300, IPC. Likewise, when the accused has beaten the son of the deceased in a quarrel and the deceased came to scold him and was struck dead, it was held that there was no fight and the act of the accused did not fall under Exception 4 to section 300, IPC.[8] The exception needs that no undue advantage be conferred of by the other side. It is not possible to say that there is no undue advantage when a man stabs an unarmed person who makes no threatening gestures and merely asks the opponent to stop fighting. Then also the fight must be with the person who is killed and not with others. In these circumstances the exception does not apply.[9]

E. Death by Consent

The last exception of section 300, IPC deals with committing death by consent which is usually known as euthanasia (mercy killing). The exception is justified on the ground that a man's life is not merely valuable to himself, but also to the family members of state and society. Therefore, a man is not entitled to capitulate his life by consent though consent has unimpeachable the effect of mitigating the potency of crime that it can never exculpate the offender.

For instance, The motives which cause a men to the commission of this offence are commonly far more respectable than those which cause a men to the commission of murder. Sometimes it is the effect of a strong sense of religious duty, sometimes of a strong sense of honour and not intermittently of humanity. The soldier who at the entreaty of a wounded comrade and keeps that comrade out of pain that the friend who grants laudanum to a person go through the torment of a lingering disease the freedman who in ancient times held out the sword that his master might fall on it and the highborn native of India who stabs the females of his family at their own entreaty in order to save them from the licentiousness of a band of freebooter it would scarcely be thought culpable.[10]

[1]Mancini v. Director of Public Prosecutions, 1942, AC 1 (9).

[2]Rex v. Lesbini,(1914) 3 KB 1116.

[3]Draft Penal Code, Note M, pp. 147, 148.

[4]Balbir Singh Balwant Singh V. The State, 1959, Cr LJ 901.

[5]Kripal Singh V. State, AIR 1951, SC 137.

[6]Dukhi Singh v. State,AIR 1955, All 379.

[7]Public Prosecutor V. Soma Sundaram, AIR 1959, Mad 323.

[8]Dandapati China V. Emperor, 1937, Mad WN 1129.

[9]Narayanan Nair V. State of Travancore-Cochin AIR 1956, SC 99.

[10]Draft Penal Code, note 4, pp. 145-146.

CHAPTER SEVEN

CONCLUSION

The interpretation of offences relating to human body are crystalline appropriate. However, both culpable homicide and murder are conjoining unassociated crimes yet and they contradict with respect to the degree of probability of death or the gravity of the act even though they seem to be corresponding in a way. It may be said that culpable homicide is a wider term than murder. If the act that is done by the offender is a execrable crime resulting in death then it drop under the yardstick of murder, insomuch, if the act leaves the victim alive with grievous hurt then it is culpable homicide which doesnot outcome in murder. Thus, in order to determine an act that the facts have to be established the first place and then knowledge and intention of the offender has to be perceived. Besides, If the intention or knowledge is higher then it would consequently come under the orbit of murder. Though, every cases are depending on the facts and circumstances and the role of judicial would be very pronounced for scrutinizing the facts thoroughly. A common line of difference is callous to be strained as there is not any exhaustive difference between section 299 and 300 IPC, it depends from case to case. Besides, the burden of presenting effective arguments before the Court will be that of the Advocates of the two parties due to facts that conclusive the level of offence.